Dog Groups

# Herding Group

by Julie Murray

2

Dash!
LEVELED READERS
An Imprint of Abdo Zoom • abdobooks.com

**Dash!**
**LEVELED READERS**

**Level 1 – Beginning**
Short and simple sentences with familiar words or patterns for children who are beginning to understand how letters and sounds go together.

**Level 2 – Emerging**
Longer words and sentences with more complex language patterns for readers who are practicing common words and letter sounds.

**Level 3 – Transitional**
More developed language and vocabulary for readers who are becoming more independent.

THIS BOOK CONTAINS RECYCLED MATERIALS

**abdobooks.com**

Published by Abdo Zoom, a division of ABDO, PO Box 398166, Minneapolis, Minnesota 55439.


Printed in the United States of America, North Mankato, Minnesota.
102023
012024

Photo Credits: Getty Images, Shutterstock
Production Contributors: Jennie Forsberg, Grace Hansen
Design Contributors: Candice Keimig, Neil Klinepier

**Library of Congress Control Number: 2023937944**

**Publisher's Cataloging in Publication Data**

Names: Murray, Julie, author.
Title: Herding group / by Julie Murray
Description: Minneapolis, Minnesota : Abdo Zoom, 2024 | Series: Dog groups | Includes online resources and index.
Identifiers: ISBN 9781098284015 (lib. bdg.) | ISBN 9781098284732 (eBook) | ISBN 9781098285098 (Read-to-Me eBook)
Subjects: LCSH: Herding dogs--Juvenile literature. | Herding behavior in animals--Juvenile literature. | Livestock protection dogs--Juvenile literature. | Dogs--Juvenile literature. | Dogs--Behavior--Juvenile literature.
Classification: DDC 636.737--dc23

# Table of Contents

Herding Group . . . . . . . . . . . . . . 4

Characteristics . . . . . . . . . . . . 12

More Herding Breeds. . . . . . . 22

Glossary . . . . . . . . . . . . . . . . . . 23

Index . . . . . . . . . . . . . . . . . . . . . 24

Online Resources . . . . . . . . . . 24

# Herding Group

German Shepherd Dog

The American Kennel Club (AKC) recognizes more than 30 **breeds** in the Herding Group.

The Herding Group was formed in 1983. It is the AKC's newest group. Before that, the **breeds** were a part of the Working Group.

Border Collie

Old English
Sheepdog

Dogs in this group were **bred** to herd livestock. Their **instinct** is to control the movement of animals.

Australian Cattle Dog

Some **breeds** in the Herding Group are used for military and police work. This is because they are natural protectors and enjoy having a job to do.

# Characteristics

Herding dogs are easy to train. They are smart and **obedient**.

Shetland Sheepdog

They herd animals in different ways. Some stare or stalk. Others bark or nip at the feet and legs of livestock.

Pembroke Welsh Corgi

Australian Shepherd

Herding dog **breeds** are energetic. They need a lot of exercise. They also love having a job to do.

They are athletic dogs that can move quickly. Many of the **breeds** perform well in **agility** competitions.

Border Collie

Herding dogs are loving and loyal. The dogs can be protective of their owners. Sometimes, they will even try to herd them!

# More Herding Breeds

Belgian Sheepdog

Bergamasco Sheepdog

Bouvier des Flandres

Briard

Mudi

Puli

# Glossary

**agility** – for dogs, a sport where one directs their dog through a pre-set obstacle course within a certain time limit.

**bred** – developed over time for a certain purpose.

**breed** – a particular type of animal.

**instinct** – natural behavior in an animal that is not taught but is simply part of what the animal is born with.

**obedient** – likely or willing to obey rules or orders.

# Index

American Kennel Club 5, 6

competition 18

exercise 17, 18

herding 9, 14, 21

intelligence 13

military 10

personality 10, 13, 17, 21

police 10

training 13

# Online Resources

Booklinks
NONFICTION NETWORK
FREE! ONLINE NONFICTION RESOURCES

To learn more about the Herding Group, please visit **abdobooklinks.com** or scan this QR code. These links are routinely monitored and updated to provide the most current information available.